I0484189

Stop The Fake It Till You Make It...A Results Driven Guide To Living Like A Real Successful Internet Marketer

7 Time-Tested Online Methods To Make Success Your New Normal

Discover How To Make Success Your New Normal In Just 7 Days From Right Now!

FREE Case Study…

I've documented every single step I took to generate $1,188.00 In just 7 days launching a very simple product on a little-known forum so you can look over my shoulder and get an insiders view of the complete process I reveal in this book.

As you read through this book, you'll get each step of the process; but, when you go to my website to get the case study, you can see me put the steps into action!

Just go to:

http://LiveTheIMLifeStyle.com

Live *The IM LifeStyle* is a website that I created because, as a reader of this book, I want to give you every opportunity to set yourself up the right way...so success will be *your* new normal!

Copyright Notice

Table of Contents

Introduction

In the following pages, you're going to discover seven simple steps that can make success *your* new normal.

I will show you how to create multiple profit centers without having a big budget, experience or technical expertise...even if all you know how to do online is send email.

I help so many people who have invested in product after product with nothing to show for it.

Struggling Entrepreneurs who have to hide their dreams, because they've failed so many times, they are starting to question whether or not they will ever breakthrough to success.

If you've tried and failed; then, tried and failed again, you will really appreciate everything I have in store for you.

Because despite your previous failed experiences, you can tap into a process where you will never have to worry about failure again. You're about to discover the power of a system that works...every time!

Rest assured, no matter how long you've been trying to make money in your own business, you are about to get the keys to your breakthrough; even if you have no mailing list, no authority and no products.

The little known but effective techniques I'll be sharing with you are designed to set you up for success from the very beginning.

Imagine what your business would be like if you had customers standing in line to buy from you, not because they know, like and trust you *like everyone is telling you*...but because you've made it impossible to say no to your offers. They want to buy from you and only you and you'll see why as you go through the pages of this book.

Let's get to it. Here are the seven steps to making success your new normal...

Chapter 1 - Finding The Pain & Pleasure

If you really want to make a significant difference, contribute to the world and make your dreams come true, then you've got to master this first step because this is where the real money is made.

Your path to success starts with solving other peoples problems. Do this right and you'll never have to worry about where your next dollar is coming from.

In this chapter, I'm going to show you how to set the foundation to make success your new normal. It begins with pain. At least, pain is the fastest route to success; but pleasure works too.

Before I tell you exactly what that means, it's important you understand why you should take this information to heart. There are a number of reasons...

First, you can take control over who you work

with day to day. All customers are not created equal so choosing the type of problems you solve will go a long way in setting up your day for fun...and profit.

That means, you don't have to deal with any customer service headaches because the people who buy from you, respect your position. This gives you the upper hand because you're offering them exactly what they need so you don't have to worry about slow sales, expensive advertising or complicated sales processes.

You see, when you help people with their pain, they look to you as an advocate, not a high pressure, sleezy salesperson.

That's why the easiest path to success is pain. Think about it. If it's not a problem, most people are not looking for the solution. On the other hand, when it is a problem, not only are people looking for the solution...they're willing to pay for that solution.

Regardless of who you are. Regardless of your experience. Regardless of the price. It's never about you...it's *always* about your customers pain.

So let's go find the pain...

Looking for problems. That's what we do.
We're Problem Solvers.

Whether you're looking to solve problems that cause pain, as I recommend...or you're looking to solve problems that move people towards pleasure. You win.

Let's say you're driving on the freeway to work. You're running late and you blow a tire. You're being interviewed for a promotion in less than three hours! Your blood boils as you pace up and down, stranded on the side of the road.

A rusted tow truck clunks by with smoke trailing in the background; then, the not-so-sane looking driver waves his hands wildly as he stops to see if you want help.

What do you do?

Do you hitch a ride so you can make it to your interview of a lifetime? Do you ask the driver if he's licensed to drive...or do you sigh with relief and thank God for sending this helpful, but crazy-looking stranger your way?

We both know the answer to that question, don't we?

But, let's take that same situation with one exception. Instead of being late for work and a potentially life changing interview, it's just a lazy Saturday afternoon so you have no time constraints...and you have a AAA Auto Club membership.

Now, what do you do?

Do you wait for the trusted AAA Tow Truck driver to show-up and tow your car into a service station...or do you go with the not so sane looking stranger?

The answer to that question is not so cut and dry, is it? I mean, you may go for the fast convenience of the strange driver, or you may wait it out listening to some tunes while you pass the time for a more trusted -- AAA Auto Service -- resource.

Can you see the difference pain makes? Yes, it's an inconvenience on the lazy Saturday afternoon, but there's no real consequence for delaying action.

This is how we define pain solutions.

Is there a major negative consequence for **not** taking action...right now?

Yes? Then that's a problem we want to look at solving.

No? Then that's a problem for another day because when you deal with pleasure solutions or solutions that would be nice and convenient but not mandatory...then you lose the sense of urgency that pain solutions deliver.

The Pain Revealed...

I have found by experience that the best way to discover the pain is to go where your potential prospects are talking about problems they want solutions to.

In one word, forums!

This is the best way to discover *the pain* so you will always have a way to create solutions...and profits with one simple Google search.

Here are the steps…

1) Go to Google and search "keyword" + forums. The keyword can be any subject where you're looking to find pains. The top three pains are health, wealth and relationships.

2) Go to each of the forums on the first three pages of Google and look for conversations, usually called forum post, where members of the forum are talking about problems they want to solve. Pay close attention to product and service questions because these type of questions indicate the person asking the question is willing to pay for the solution to their problem.

3) Make a list of all the questions where members are willing to pay for the solution. Pick three of those questions that are the most interesting to you so you can enjoy the process while you're solving the problem.

That's it! You've just completed the first step! Don't let the simplicity of the above three steps fool you. These steps are simple, but powerful.

Now, as you go through this process you may get stuck wondering is the problem you're looking at a big enough problem so people will pay for the solution.

No need to second-guess yourself. If you find three to five forum members using different words to ask the same question, then you've found a problem worth paying for.

The great thing about this process is the fact -- no matter what you do -- all your work will pay off! It will pay off in sales. It will pay off in getting customers that will buy from you over and over again. It will pay off because you are building assets that take a little time to build once...but pay you dividends...for life!

And, that's just the beginning.

Now, that you've got burning problems where people are willing to pay to get rid of their pains. How do you turn these problems into solutions? You're about to find out in the next

Chapter 2 - Digging For Gold On Google

You've just completed the hardest part. Now we're going to take those problems and find solutions that people are willing to pay for.

As you're about to see this really is the easy part because all the heavy lifting has been done for you. You see, there are already products and services that exist that solve your prospects pain.

Unfortunately, those products and services are usually too expensive, sound like scams or just don't *talk the right way* to your prospects so they want to buy.

Your research for the solution to your prospects problems is vital because you don't want to make the same mistakes your competition is making.

This is why you want to take control of what you present to your prospects from the very beginning. This is not a hit and miss process. This is about precision.

After this research process, your prospects will feel like you can read their minds and they will buy from you because you understand them so well that it doesn't feel like they're being sold. It feels like they're being helped...because that's what you're doing - helping them.

You will see your efforts pay off every time you get the email notification that you've made another sale.

You will see your efforts pay off every time you get an email from a customer thanking you for helping them out of their pain.

You will see your efforts pay off every time you see all the buyers on your email list opening your emails because they want to hear from you and they're waiting...with credit card in hand to buy from you, again!

I first discovered the power of researching solutions that people are willing to pay for when I was just 12 years old.

Yep. Still in middle school chatting on Yahoo when a business person, a real adult, looking for help...paid me to make her a banner ad. Me, a 12 year old kid!

And that's when I understood that making money is really about putting the right offer in front of the right people.

But, I'm getting ahead of myself because it really starts with paying attention to what people already want, what people are already looking to buy and getting in front of those people.

Again, three simple steps...then you've got the solution people are willing to pay good money for.

1) Google the three questions you found on the forums where people are looking to pay for solutions to their problems

2) Write down the first five websites you come to that have products and/or services that answer the questions to

those problems

3) Break-down the sales messages for each of the five websites into three categories. Category one, list all the bullet points for each website. Category two, list each of the irresistible offers for each website; and, Category three, list all the benefits & unique characteristics for each website.

You've just completed the core research necessary to create a product that people are looking for...and want to buy. So all you need to do now is take that research to create your own product and irresistible offer!

The biggest hurdle most new product creators have when starting this process is... believing there's an issue -- an ethical issue -- with stealing other peoples work.

You can relax because you are not stealing. You are simply swiping the proven sales data of other product creators to develop your own new *original* product.

This means you don't have to struggle through

traditional testing and failing procedures because you are working from a proven framework A framework of websites that are already selling products to your prospects.

Basically, you are coming in, taking the best of the best...and helping people on an even higher level.

Even better than that, you get to go from idea to product with a simple three-hour process that you'll discover in the next chapter!

Let's begin...

Chapter 3 - Transcription Products & Profits On Demand

The power of this chapter comes from the fact you can create a brand new product, without writing a single word, without speaking english and without any technical expertise in just three-hours...or less!

Which makes this great for internationals who

speak languages outside of english, english is the second language or for people who just don't have the time to sit down and create a product on their own.

Bottom line, if you can speak, you can create a product anywhere in the world, on any schedule and in any language.

This means you have no limitations. You don't have to depend on someone else to give you permission to do what you're already burning inside to do.

You've already done the research so now, all you have to do is get your research into a format to help as many people as possible.

Because the more people you help...the more money you make, the more freedom you have and the more relevant you are to the world.

I see so many would be successful entrepreneurs stuck in the struggle because they miss out on getting this one part right.

You don't have to do everything yourself. In fact, if you just record a short message, you can create a product people will stand in line to buy.

Three Steps To Success...

It's really very simple. Follow the below three steps and you can have a completed special report product by the end of today!

Here are the steps...

1) Take your research to make an outline of how you are going to solve the problem you researched

2) Call into your own phone number to record a voicemail message where you ask and answer each part of your outline, yourself.

   You can do this in one sitting, over a few days or you can just record a conversation where you have a friend ask you the questions from your outline.

3) Have your recording professionally transcribed & that transcription will become the manuscript for your product.

Do you remember when I told you the first step, finding the pain, is the hardest step? That's the hardest step because you have to take what you learned and actually do something; however, this third step is the most challenging because you will come head to head with self-limiting beliefs that tell you...

- You don't have anything to say

- You're not good enough

- No one will listen to you

Of course, none of the above statements are true; however, we all battle with these thoughts because it's human nature to challenge anything that attempts to fundamentally change who we are.

And, through this product creation process...*you will change*.

Instead of producing value for your time through wages, you're producing value for one-off use of your time because you get paid over and over again for each product creation.

Instead of someone outside of yourself determining how much you deserve to get paid, you decide that for yourself; and, you validate your decision by creating an offer that makes it easy for prospects to say yes...to whatever price you demand.

Most can't handle the responsibility of that type of change, which is why most will give up before they even get started.

But, you are not like most...

I know this because you've read this far...and you're going to keep reading until you finish this book and then you're going to make a key decision.

We'll talk more about that decision in a moment but first, let me tell you this...

Now, that you know the only thing that can hold you back is human nature, you have everything you need to overcome your obstacles because with this knowledge, comes the power to fight the internal struggle of change.

Break through this natural barrier and you'll be

more than ready for the next step.

What's the next step?

Glad you asked;-) Let's turn your new product into cash-flow with one simple document that can upgrade any financial situation into prosperity.

Chapter 4 - Proven Sales Template That Works Every Time For ANY Offer

In this chapter, I'm going to show you how to create a sales message that can be used to create written sales letters, video sales letters, teleseminars and any other medium of sales message distribution.

However, first it's important you understand that you can create a powerful sales message without being a guru and without testimonials; heck, you don't even need a finished product!

Remember the foundational rule: It's not about you.

It's about your customer and their pains...and desires. When you speak their language, in the form of your sales message, it's like you're reading their mind.

Even better than that, you're not just connecting with them through empathy, but you're offering them a real solution to their problem.

A solution that's not available anywhere else!

This means you get to take control of a sales process that pretty much guarantees success because you've created an exclusive product based on what the customer already wants.

Can you imagine how good it'll feel when the product you created is bringing you sales everyday? Even better than that, think of all the people you get to help.

This is the type of business where you instantly earn the respect of your friends, family and co-workers because they see you producing products that actually help people!

Plus, your sales message puts you on the

other side of the cash register. And, that's where you belong because you don't buy opportunity, you create it.

Product creation is what we covered in the first three chapters; and, now we're going to use all your research to create a sales message that'll have the right prospects lined up to buy from you.

Here are the five simple steps to creating a sales message that compels your prospects to buy…

1. ***Big Promise...***

   You make a statement of how you're going to help your prospects get rid of the pain you researched in the first step. Keep it simple, like…

   a. How To Stop (pain) In 3 Simple Steps Without (objection)

   b. 5 Easy Steps To Being (pain)-Free Without (objection)

   c. How To Get (desire) In Just

3-Days...Even If (objection)

    i.   Objections are time, money, and resources

2. ***Tease Big Promise With Bullet Points...***

You want to take three to five bullet points from each of the sales pages you discovered during your research; and rewrite those bullet points -- in your own words -- for your own product.

3. ***Explain Offer + Scarcity...***

An offer is simply what your prospects are going to receive after they buy your product or service.

This could be a written report, audio mp3, physical product, coaching, infographics, membership access, etc.

Combine what your customers are going to receive with an action trigger called scarcity (set time/quantity limitations)...and you've got a sales message that works!

4. **Risk Reversal...**

You want to reverse the risk from your prospects. Put all the risk on your own shoulders...with a money back guarantee.

Basically, when you make a strong guarantee, you win and your customer wins because they can buy with confidence...and you get a sale that you may have lost without the guarantee!

5. **Call To Action (CTA)...**

You've got to tell your prospects exactly what to do. If you don't tell -- not ask -- them to buy, then you leave it up to them to make a decision...without a directive to make *the right decision*.

Don't assume you're prospects will click the buy button simply because it's there. If you don't tell them what to do, they just may devour your sales message...then leave empty handed.

Five simple steps...that's it! You've just discovered the best way to create a sales message that works everytime!

The only thing that'll hold you back is thinking you need to do more & look more like the gurus with all their fancy doodads.

You know what I mean; videos, testimonials, overwhelming bonuses, and so on...but the truth is, while those things may be *nice*, they are not *necessary*.

Don't hold yourself back from success by trying to keep up with the gurus. They have a staff to do all that *nice but unnecessary* stuff. We need to use our time, money and resources to be more efficient, not wasteful...and just focus on the stuff that matters.

When you get your sales message together, as shown above, and put it in any medium: videos, blog post, written sales pages, etc., then you can sell anything, anytime, anywhere *and* create cash out of thin air!

Now, if you want to put this process on steroids, you'll want to pay close attention to the next chapter.

Chapter 5 - Mafia Product Launch

This chapter is just fun! You get to take all your hard work & notch it up another level!

The Mafia Product Launch is all about giving your customers **more** than the solution to their problem! You give them something they really, really want...something they want so bad, they would buy your product just to get this *extra special* bonus.

Now, this isn't about selling your soul and giving so much away that you're trapped under the weight of your product launch for months to come.

This is about being strategic and developing a little something extra that your prospects would crawl over broken glass to get to!

Do you remember the Sport Illustrated Super

Bowl commercials? They used to give away these ugly football phones to sports fans who accepted a free trial offer to their magazine.

Have you ever received an offer for a **free** vacation including airfare, room and board...simply for checking out a timeshare presentation?

Do you remember Oprah's favorite things, where she gave away premium products to her audience...like the free Ford Taurus?

Well, those are what you call Mafia Product Launch Bonuses. The best way to create your own mafia offers is to get a little creative and follow the three step method below...

1. Take the unique selling points from each of the sales pages you discovered during your research

2. Brainstorm ways you can combine two or three of those unique selling points into one unique offer

3. Describe your new unique offer, using the words of your best potential

customers, to increase the value of your product.

How do you use their words? Easy. Just look at those sales pages again to check out the testimonials...and match the exact tone of the testimonials to describe your Mafia Product Launch Bonus!

You will see the power of this strategy payoff immediately. Sales gush in because your bonus is so unique...so creative...and so desired, that your prospects are compelled to buy!

Not only will your sales instantly skyrocket, but your new customers will have such an amazing experience, they'll tell their friends and other connections all about your great promotion!

You may have one challenge to overcome and that's thinking you're bonus isn't grand enough. Most of us are not Oprah...and we don't have to be. That's the reason I gave the Sports Illustrated example.

You see, the Sports Illustrated people put their offer in front of football fans...and that's why their offer worked. As long as your offer is something your ideal customers want, then you're in great shape.

Don't worry about grand over the top bonuses; instead, focus on bonuses that are unique, desired and relevant to the people who are checking out your sales message.

Get this right and your product launches will be a huge success so you'll always know exactly where your next sales are coming from.

Of course, now that you've got all these paying customers, you've got to treat them right **and** manage their expectations. They need to know you're in their corner and you will continue to help them...way beyond the initial sale.

Chapter 6 - Ongoing Customer Satisfaction & Sales Set-Ups

When a prospects separates themselves from their money to invest in your products and services, they are making a statement of trust...in you!

At this point, delivering on your promises maintains that trust; but, you want to do more than maintain trust, you want to increase trust so you can set-up the next offer in such a way your new customer is going to buy, simply because *you* made the offer.

This is important because initially your prospect buys because of what you have to say in your sales message; however, once the prospect becomes a customer...and you increase the level of trust through product delivery, then your prospect buys because of their connection with you…

This is the kind of power every entrepreneur

looks for because when people buy from you because they trust you, they will continue to buy over and over again.

You know what that means?

That means, you get to increase your income...on demand, simply by delivering on every promise you make... through product delivery.

No extra work because you're going to deliver the product anyway. No extra time because you set your product delivery up in a way that gives your customer a great customer experience. No additional cost because you're making more profits from repeat buyers so you can invest a little more in creating great user experiences for your customers!

Here's five different ways you can create a better user experience...

1. On going support through Skype, Facebook or your own membership site

2. Unadvertised bonus(es)

3. Free coaching critiques

4. Direct mail: certificates of completion, trophies, CDs, etc.

5. Manage expectations

Most of the above are self-explanatory; however, I want to expand a little on the last recommendation, managing expectations.

Southwest Airlines has a saying, "Customers will accept anything, if you manage their expectations." Southwest offers cheap flying rates, small seating and peanuts, no meals, for a snack. Their customers know this, and their customers are satisfied because their expectations have been managed.

Southwest customers are not expecting big comfortable seats, great snack selection or even the best service...because their expectations have been managed.

If you streamline your process to the basics, promote the basics. Don't promote you have all the bells and whistles when you offer a functional service.

If you have five customized options, promote those options. Don't promote personalization as a key selling point...if it's not an option.

Let me give you an example. If you go to Kunaki.com, you will find a CD duplication service that is simple, yet functional with minimal customer service. They are upfront about what they offer...and customers love their simple process.

Decide on what you will and won't do...then promote your limitations, restrictions and abilities as benefits! **Everything** you do is a benefit to your customers, the right customers, so make sure you are managing their expectations based on your own business practices, not your competitive environment.

The final key to managing expectations is consistency. When we go to McDonalds, we know what to expect; and if you want your customers to keep coming back for more, you'll want to be consistent with your all your communications.

After you've gone through this process a few times, you'll probably want to take a step up and scale your business to even higher levels of success.

The best way to scale your business is to outsource some...or all of the moving parts. You do this through leverage, as you'll see in the next chapter.

Chapter 7 - Outsourcing: Rinse & Repeat Profits

If you skipped to this chapter because you want to have someone else do all the work for you, while you do little or nothing, then you're putting yourself at a disadvantage.
Because if you have not done the process yourself, you will miss out on some key distinctions. Distinctions only discovered when you do the work.

Remember, this is about scaling through leverage. If you have not gone through the process yourself, how are you going to help your outsourcers when they need help? How will you know what skills are needed to do the job most effectively...and efficiently? How will you know if a process can be changed to be more profitable to your bottom line?

The answer to those questions is, you won't know...and that's why you're putting you and your outsourcers at a disadvantage when you miss out on the key foundational experience you get from doing this process yourself.

Now, if you have gone through the process and done the work, get ready for multiple streams of cash-flow because you can have this process done for you, over and over again, at no cost to you!

How? Let me explain...

You see, the first time you go through this process, you will have some minimal expenses...all of which should be recouped with your first few sales.

Anyway, the first time around, you're just getting your feet wet; but, after you've had this experience, you will know exactly what to expect.

That means, you can outsource each step of the *entire* process and let other people do the heavy lifting while you sit back...and get paid!

It's like you become an instant franchise. However, instead of sharing your profits with the franchisees, you get to keep all the profits, reinvest a little of those profits -- each time -- so you are virtually creating new income streams, at no additional cost to you!

And, this is your biggest advantage. You've tapped into a process that's been proven -- by a 12 year old, no less -- to work...every single time, in every market.

It's like you get to create new profit centers over and over again...then, rinse & repeat your way to financial independence!

Each profit center is independent giving you a new source of income, customers and portfolio of assets.

Can you see how this will give you the freedom to work when you want to work, take vacations without worry of bills and debt hanging over

your head, and buy what you want to buy...
without having to check your bank account?

This type of scaling through leverage of other
peoples time, skillsets and resources is the
strategy that can make success your new
normal.

Just follow these outsourcing guidelines and
you'll be on the right path...

1. Break each of the product creation steps
   down into smaller tasks because
   outsourcers can typically do *one* thing
   really well.

2. Contract three outsourcers at a time to
   do one specific task. This will give you a
   frame of reference for what you should
   expect from qualified outsourcers.

3. Once you have a team of outsourcers,
   you can pretty much automate the entire
   process so it can run without you!

The most difficult part of leveraging your
business using outsourcing is accepting the

realities of outsourcing. You can outsource different task; however, you cannot outsource thinking. **You** bring the creative force to your business...and outsourcers bring your thoughts into reality.

It is a myth that you can outsource complicated processes for two or three bucks an hour. If you follow the steps above, you will have a more realistic view and a better experience of outsourcing because you won't have unrealistic expectations.

After you've been at this outsourcing game for a while, it will be hard to imagine your life without it. So press through the initial, yet minor frustrations...and success will be your new normal.

Summary Conclusion

We've come a long way. I've shown you how to find pains that people are willing to pay to get solved. How to research so you can create a product that prospects want to buy...and how to create that product.

I showed you how to create a sales message and mafia bonus so prospects are compelled to buy your products.

I've also shown you how to increase customer trust so they buy more from you...simply because you manage their expectations

Finally, I showed you how to scale the entire process so you can have others do all the heavy lifting for you...so success can be your new normal.

Understand that I stumbled upon the basics of this process when I was just 12-years old...and I've improved upon it, each year, for the last fifteen years.

That means, if a 12-year old kid can do this simple process, so can you. Now, if you want my help, I'm here to help you.

In fact, after I've helped you build your first few profit centers, you may want to go to the next level & let me help you create your own coaching program!

In closing, I hope you enjoyed reading this

book as much as I enjoyed putting it together for you.

And just one more thing…

If you did enjoy reading this book as much as I enjoyed creating it for you, will you pay it forward by writing a review of this book to let others know the benefits you received from reading it?

This will not only help others get refocused so they can make success their new normal too, but it's incredibly rewarding for me to know how much my work is helping others.

You can leave a review by going to:
http://www.amazon.com/dp/B00SGV086G

Thank you in advance for your support:-)